GOD OF THE SANDPIT

50 PRAYERS FOR CHILDREN, YOUNG PEOPLE, SCHOOL STAFFS AND THEIR CHRISTIAN SCHOOL COMMUNITIES

Rachele and Gabby Tullio

MOSAIC PRESS

Published in Australia by
Mosaic Press
508 High St
Preston Vic. 3072
Australia

Mosaic Press is an imprint of Mosaic Resources Pty Ltd

ISBN 9781743241011

First published 2013

Cataloguing-in-Publication entry is available for the National Library of Australia http:/catalogue.nla.gov.au/.

Book design by John Healy
Printed and bound in Great Britain by
Marston Book Services Limited, Oxfordshire

CONTENTS

FOREWORD

I am delighted to have the opportunity to provide a foreword for the book *God of the Sandpit*, which is authored by Rachele and Gabby Tullio. I have known Rachele and Gabby since I became Archbishop of Adelaide and my knowledge of them has led me to see just how committed they are to the life of our Church as well as how talented they are in their ability to influence others by leading them to deeper and deeper experiences of prayer.

I think that this book will be a great help to Families, Schools and young Catholics all over our Country to deepen the bonds between themselves and our Lord, as well as our connection to the life of our Church, which is so necessary in the midst of the exciting times in which we live today. By exciting times, I mean times that can actually make it difficult for people to focus on the relationship that we all should have with Christ and the Church. These exciting times mean that there are so many elements of our current lifestyles that can attract us away from the Lord, because of the false hope that is offered to us by the circumstances of this society. Often the subtle messages of the noises that surround us can distract us and convince us in our heart of hearts that we will truly find our peace and joy in other elements of the world and universe that we are a part of.

Rachele and Gabby have the great ability to be able to see how in the midst of all that excitement, it is possible for people who lead a busy life to have a meaningful living relationship with the Lord which they express through prayer. I know that this book will be a great aid to many people, from Families to School Staff, in that regard.

So, I wholeheartedly endorse *God of the Sandpit* and pray that many people, in opening it, will discover not just the experience of prayer, but the experience of the Lord.

+ Philip Wilson.

Most Rev Philip Wilson DD JCL
Archbishop of Adelaide

INTRODUCTION

Many years ago, we were inspired to create a unique collection of prayers that 'spoke' to teachers and students of a loving God. This collection of prayer has been carefully crafted with young people, school staff and prayer communities in mind as they explore a meaningful relationship with God. Topics include the spirituality of children, young people in search of meaning, the mission of Jesus, God and social justice, the spirituality of teaching, the seeking of wisdom (named as the Holy Spirit) and communities celebrating important school-based events.

Our prayers are engaging and relevant to school staff and to the wider community, setting them apart from other school prayer resources. They use contemporary language and imaginative settings that enhance an understanding of a loving and compassionate God.

We believe this prayer resource will reaffirm the spirituality of children, young people, school staff and the wider Catholic school community, supporting the central place of prayer in Catholic schools. Our prayers include short wisdom stories, appropriate Scripture and reflections for staff meetings, parent gatherings, School Boards and school assemblies. The collection is also an ideal resource for parishes, retreat centres, families or any groups that gather to pray.

The approach to prayer taken in this book is to help people pray with meaning. How?

- Our prayers name the questions of the heart to God.
- Our prayers reflect on decision-making based on Scripture.
- Our prayers express gratitude to God for the wonder and mystery of life.

Gabby and Rachele Tullio

Gabby and Rachele Tullio have worked extensively with children, young people and staff in Catholic schools.

1. PRAYER OF A CHILD

Dear God,
I am a child.
I know everything there is to know about playgrounds and sandpits.
They are my territory; they are places that help my sense of adventure and my sense of wonder.
My days are simple, Lord, because I am young.
I am innocent of life's complexities and dangers.
For You, Lord, have given me what I need to understand life at this tender age.
I can sense immediately those who care for me.
Sometimes, I act awkwardly when I feel I cannot achieve what is expected of me.
Occasionally my stubbornness gets in the way of my trying something new.
It is easy to forget I am only a child.
Lord, as I grow, I have heard whispers that my time of childhood will not last long:
- that my fascination with butterflies and flowers will disappear.
- that I will begin to be fussy about playing with other children.
- that my trust in You will weaken.

I hope this is not true, God.
I will always love what You create and the beauty that surrounds me.
I will always enjoy my time with my young friends, even if we struggle to understand each other some days.
I will always look for You and talk with You, God, even when I am bigger and older.
You have probably heard this all before from other children long ago.
But what I need from You, God, are the people in my life who believe in You as much as I do.
'Cause only then will I grow in 'faith and hope and love'.
And even if I am young, my heart tells me that the greatest of these is: 'love'....another name I give You, God.

Amen.

2. GOD OF THE SANDPIT

God of endless chattering children
God of stubborn toddlers.
God of wondering moments.
God of wailing cries.
God of cherished, precious silence.
God of young, bossy personalities.
God of non-stop questioning
God of intrigued stares.
God of cuddling pets.
God of mourning dead flowers.
God of green vegetables.
God of crust-less sandwiches.
God of sensitive children.
God of mumbling children.
God of giggling children.
God of children who don't give up or give in.
God of reasonable children who have unreasonable moments.
God of children who say incredibly cute things
And say incredibly silly things.
God of wonder.
God of awe.
You made them all.
You made children in Your image and likeness.
Bless all children.
For You made them all with love.

Amen.

3. BLESSED ARE THE CHILDREN

Blessed are the children who sleep peacefully during the night.
Blessed are the children whose toothless smiles light up faces.
Blessed are the quiet children, the chatterers and the questioners.
Blessed are those children who do as they are told.
Blessed are the children who say 'sorry' and mean it.
Blessed are those children who are grateful for what they have.
Blessed are those who enjoy tickle-fights and funny jokes.
Blessed are the adventurers who are always covered in mud.
Blessed are the whispering children and all those with loud voices.
Blessed are the compliant ones who make a parent's day easier.
Blessed are the uncooperative children who spend time-out in their rooms.
Blessed are the cheeky children who give smart answers.
Blessed are the sensible children and those with sensitive personalities.
Blessed are the children who should know better and don't always choose this wisdom.
Blessed are the children who choose peace over fighting.
Blessed are those who include other children in play.
Blessed are those children who are fair,
- who have hope.
- who have dreams.
- who believe in God.
We give thanks to God for children who inspire us and enable us
to see the world through eyes of potential: through God's eyes.
We pray for children who struggle to bring their potential to their world.
May they receive God's Blessings and strength
as they grow into the beautiful people
God knows they are capable of becoming.

Amen.

4. I AM A CHILD

I am a child, Lord.
My world is challenging as I learn how:
 to use a spoon,
 tie up my shoelaces
 put away my toys.
I question everything adults do and know how to exasperate them with my question of "why"?
Most times I do this innocently.
The world seems really, really big to me; at times I am totally overwhelmed by it.
Occasionally I become stubborn and refuse to give in.
I need Your assurance, Lord, about growing up. This is what I think:

I will learn about how things grow and change; but I also need to learn how to welcome life and farewell it too.

I will learn how to make new friends; but I also need to learn that it is okay to treasure the old ones just as much.

I will learn how to share my toys, my games and my feelings; but I also need to learn how to express this respectfully.

There is so much to learn, God, that I need You near me every day.
Thank you for the care that people give me during my journey of learning.
They make it better for me to grow into the magnificent human being we **both** know I am meant to be.

Amen.

SCRIPTURE: 1 Thessalonians 2:7-8, 11-12

Just as a mother cares for her children, so we cared for you. Because we loved you so much, we were delighted to share with you not only the gospel of God but our lives as well.
For you know that we dealt with each of you as a parent deals with their own who calls you into his kingdom and glory.

Leader: The Word of the Lord.
All: **Thanks be to God.**

5. BECAUSE I SAID SO...

The response is: ***Because I said so...***

Leader: Jesus, I am surrounded by children for most of my day. At times, I feel challenged to keep calm when they ask me too many questions at once. Thank you, Lord, for inspiring me with the perfect response for children when this happens. Some days, their constant question of 'why?' exasperates me. My best answer becomes: 'Because I said so...'

Allow me to share with You, Lord, the challenges I face some days with them:

"Why do I have to go to bed now? It's early!"

Response: ***Because I said so.***

"I don't like the green bits in my food. Why do I have to eat it?'

Response: ***Because I said so.***

"Why do I have to clean up my little cousin's mess? She did it too!"

Response: ***Because I said so.***

"No-body goes to Church anymore. Why do I have to go?"

Response: ***Because I said so.***

"Why can't I go to the party? You haven't told me why!"

Response: ***Because I said so.***

"Why can't I wear this?"

Response: ***Because I said so.***

Leader: Jesus, I know that I sometimes overuse this response with children. You and I both know how clever they can be at 'pushing buttons' and getting this answer.

Jesus, when I have space to think things through, I feel better. 'Because I said so' lets them know that I have values that I treasure. They are important to me.

Help me not to forget that my task in their lives is to keep communicating what I value and what I am prepared to defend.

Give me the strength to always do this with You as my support and with You as their example.

Amen.

6. 'ARE WE THERE YET?'

The car was all loaded up and ready to go.
It was holiday time with the kids!
As the last child clicked in the seatbelt, it started.
"Leave me alone!"
"Don't talk to me!"
"Give it back!'
"Go away!"
"Don't look at me!"
"No!"
"Don't touch my stuff!"
"I'm thirsty!"
"I'm hungry!"
"I'm tired!"
"Move over!"
"Don't talk to me!"
"Stop it!!!!"
"Are we there yet?"
Pity was, the car hadn't even been started yet. They were still at home.

PRAYER

Lord of adults and of children. Lord of patience and forgiveness.
Lord of tenderness and understanding. Lord of miracles and strength.
Lord of stillness and compassion. Lord of all.
In moments that I need Your Presence in my life, remind me that You are with me in all situations.

Amen.

7. OUR MEETING PRAYER

Leader: We welcome all those who have come to this meeting in the spirit of God's peace. Let us begin with the sign of the Cross: in the name of the Father, and of the Son and of the Holy Spirit.
All: **Amen**

Leader: Prayer can guide us to make choices. Prayer puts our needs before God first as we bring to God our concerns. When we thank God in prayer, we acknowledge that all is well and we are at peace.

Leader: Our faith, our prayers and our spirituality shape our attitudes. They help us to name or to be aware of what is important in our life. We ask God to give us the ability to distinguish between what we seek and what we need in life and to give us this same ability for the well-being of this group.
All: Lord, we bring before You an agenda that is important to us and to many. Give us the capacity to work through the many issues that it may bring, Lord, so we can discuss them amicably and cooperatively in the Spirit of Your Truth

Amen.

SCRIPTURE: **Psalm 40:4-8**

Blessed is the one who trusts in the Lord.
Many, Lord, my God, are the wonders You have done, the things You planned for us.
None can compare with You; were I to speak and tell of Your deeds, they would be too many to declare.
Sacrifice and offering You did not desire— but my ears You have opened— burnt offerings and sin offerings You did not require.
Then I said, "Here I am, I have come— it is written about me in the scroll.
I desire to do Your will, my God; Your law is within my heart."

The Word of the Lord.
All: **Thanks be to God**

8. THE ROAD OF LIFE

Your journey is just beginning.
As you travel the road of life, be gentle with yourself.
Do not permit the small pebbles under your feet to determine your way or your feelings.
They have the potential to grow in your imagination: remember they are just pebbles.
Enjoy the gentle breezes that cool and refresh you on the journey.
But wisely take shelter off the road when these gusts turn into fierce winds.
Protect yourself in a strong place and wait for the storm to pass.
Know that it always will.
Allow the sun to warm your skin but be mindful of this: too much of a good thing can also burn you.
Enjoy the solitude, and at the same time, the company of your journey.
The journey has its own moments that will teach you something.
Take the time to notice the beauty that surrounds you.
It has been with you all the time – notice it and give into it, now and then.
Don't rush. Rest when you need it. It will give you perspective.
Reflect often.
Be grateful often.
Forgive often. For these things add meaning on the road you are travelling.
But most importantly, have courage on the journey- be it long or short.
For the road is uniquely yours and… ***I am always with you.*** **God.**

9. THE SILENT SHOUT - GOOD FRIDAY

It was a terrible scene. Many could not look at it.
In pain, Jesus heard the crowd shouting obscenities at him.
He remained silent and did not respond.
Suddenly, because of his silent dignity, the mood changed.
Some people were strangely moved by his silence.
As they looked at Jesus, they began to wonder....
Suddenly, their hearts were filled with compassion.
Many were moved to tears
There was a deafening silence as all gazed at the Lord.
The point is... in God's case... ***you don't have to shout to be heard.***

THOUGHTS

God does not shout to be heard.
Shouting doesn't validate a message.
Only Truth does.
And Truth speaks in gentle whispers to the heart...even in silence.
This is how God is heard.
With an open heart.

SCRIPTURE: Luke 23:44-49

It was now about noon, and darkness came over the whole land until three in the afternoon, for the sun stopped shining. And the curtain of the temple was torn in two. Jesus called out with a loud voice, "Father, into your hands I commit my spirit." When he had said this, he breathed his last.
The centurion, seeing what had happened, praised God and said, "Surely this was a righteous man."
When all the people who had gathered to witness this sight saw what took place, they beat their breasts and went away. But all those who knew him, including the women who had followed him from Galilee, stood at a distance, watching these things.

The Gospel of the Lord.
All: **Praise to you Lord Jesus Christ**.

10. A THINKING HEART

The young man was on a quest.
He was seeking wisdom.
Dissatisfied with his life, he did not find it in his technologies.
He did not find it in his peers.
So he went far away looking far looking for wisdom.
Eventually he came across a wise old man.
"Tell me how to find wisdom," he asked the old man.
There was a pause. The wise old man eventually spoke slowly and steadily..
"Wisdom," he began softly, "is thinking with the heart of God."
The young man thought about it deeply.
He went away satisfied.

SCRIPTURE: Proverbs 10:2, 8, 9, 12, 19

Here are some proverbs from a wisdom figure called Solomon.

Ill-gotten treasures have no lasting value,
but righteousness delivers from death.
The wise in heart accept commands,
but a chattering fool comes to ruin.
Whoever walks in integrity walks securely,
but whoever takes crooked paths will be found out.
Hatred stirs up conflict,
but love covers over all wrongs.
Sin is not ended by multiplying words,
but the prudent hold their tongues.

The Word of the Lord
All: **Thanks be to God.**

11. RECOGNISING GOD

Jesus decided to see whether or not people would recognise him.
He became the face of a happy child… then an encouraging word, then a humorous comment… then a difficult discussion… then a life-giving moment… then some timely advice... and the face of hope.

Jesus was not recognised sometimes by others during the course of the day.
….But Jesus recognised them…

THOUGHTS

God's face can be seen often.
…in the face of others and in what they say and do out of compassion…
But especially in the face of those who care.

PRAYER

Lord, thank you for Your Presence in our lives. At times it is hard to recognise Your words that speak to us through different people.
We know that You care about us deeply and that You are always ready to encourage and protect us.
Help us to be mindful of Your Presence each day.

Amen.

SCRIPTURE: Exodus 3:7-9 (adapted)

The Lord said, "I have indeed seen the misery of my people…
I have heard them crying out… and I am concerned about their suffering.
So I have come down to rescue them …and to bring them up out of that land into a good and spacious land... ***my*** people..."

Leader: The Word of the Lord.
All: **Thanks be to God.**

12. GOING ORGANIC AND STAYING HEALTHY

They were trying hard to eat well and stay healthy.
Everything they ate was certified 'organic'.
Not a single chemical or pesticide was on their food.
Only what was healthy was eaten.
But their spiritual lives were unhealthy….
In the end, it didn't matter what kind of healthy stuff went into their bodies.
What mattered to God was what came out…of their hearts

THOUGHTS

God cares about how we take care of our bodies.
God cares even more about how we take care of our souls.
Nothing can destroy the soul – but the condition of the soul is another matter.
We are asked to look after our soul's condition by thinking, being and doing 'healthy' as God want us to …certified organic or not.

SCRIPTURE: Mark 7:14-21

Again Jesus called the crowd to him and said, "Listen to me, everyone, and understand this. Nothing outside a person can defile them by going into them. Rather, it is what comes out of a person that defiles them."
After he had left the crowd and entered the house, his disciples asked him about this parable. "Are you so dull?" he asked. "Don't you see that nothing that enters a person from the outside can defile them? For it doesn't go into their heart but into their stomach, and then out of the body." (In saying this, Jesus declared all foods clean.)
He went on: "What comes out of a person is what defiles them. For it is from within, out of a person's heart, that evil thoughts come.

Leader: The Gospel of the Lord.
All: **Praise to you, Lord Jesus Christ**.

13. MY CHILD

One day, a grateful parent wanted to share some important information about their child with God.
"Lord," they began, "there is no one more precious than my child.
My child can say the most impressive things.
My child can engage in the most charming conversations with others.
My child can be absolutely brilliant!
I am often in awe of how clever my child is."
The parent continued to point out all the wonderful qualities of their child.
The Lord listened respectfully as the parent explained all the child's gifts and talents.
Finally, the Lord spoke.
"Just remember, you are My child too. And so is every other person in the world..."
And suddenly, the parent understood how God feels about **us.**

THOUGHTS

- God has no favourites.
- As we grow, God is totally interested in us.
- God delights in our gifts and talents.
- The hard part is sometimes believing it the way God does.

SCRIPTURE: Letter to the Ephesians 3:17

"...I pray that you, being grounded and established in love, may have power, together with all the Lord's holy people, to grasp how wide and long and high and deep is the love of Christ, and to know this love that surpasses all knowledge—that you may be filled to the measure of all, the fullness of God."

Amen.

14. THE RAINBOW

The child was awestruck by the beautiful rainbow.
The deep, intense colours stretched out across a sky of grey clouds.
God happened to be passing by, but the child was engrossed in the beauty of the rainbow and didn't notice the Lord.
God gently coughed to get some attention
The child still didn't notice God.
God gently whispered 'hello' in the child's ear.
But still the child didn't realise God was near.
And then God realised something!
"What a beautiful rainbow," said God, sitting close to the child.
And together they stared at its majesty.
"Yes, it is," replied the child absently and then turned to God and asked, "Will you stay and watch it with me?"
God nodded.
Together they stared at the rainbow in silence.
The moment was called **'sacred'**.
It needed no words…or justification.

SCRIPTURE: Matthew 11:25

At that time Jesus said:
"I praise you, Father, Lord of heaven and earth, because You have hidden these things from the wise and learned and revealed them to little children."

The Gospel of the Lord.
All: **Praise to you, Lord Jesus Christ**.

15. THE CHILD'S WORLD

Don't run – you'll fall!
Careful you don't cut yourself!
Give it back – now!
Don't put it too close to the edge – it will fall and break!
Leave it alone!
Put it back!
Close it!
Open it!
Don't move!
Move it!
And?
Who told you?
When did *that* happen?
Because I say so!
Hurry up!
Tell me the truth!
Remember, that our conversations with children are *blessings in disguise.* Our conversations with God are disguises in blessings. God blesses us through the love we have for others and through the love we receive from others. This is what Jesus taught us.

PRAYER

Lord, we thank you for the gift of children. They are treasures of the world because they were created to be a hope for the future. Yet we know that not all children in the world have the same care and dignity that is Your dream for them.

We remember children who are homeless. We remember children who are alone and fearful of the future. We remember children who are caught up in conflicts whether in their homes or in their countries. We remember children who have forgotten how to play. Give us the strength to be their voice of justice in the world. For Your love of children is carried in Your heart, Lord. **Amen.**

16. TOO MUCH OF ANYTHING

Too much worrying.
Too much crying.
Too much criticising.
Too much seriousness.
Too much working.
Too much arguing.
Too much of anything…is stressful.
Too much of anything can consume us and becomes a burden.
God does not want us to be worn down with burdens.
Handing over the burdens to God is the start of "less"…
Less worrying.
Less crying.
Less criticising.
Less working.
Less stress….
Stress…less.
Too much of anything that consumes us really becomes ***less*** of everything.

SCRIPTURE: Proverbs 27:19

As water reflects the face, so one's life reflects the heart.

PRAYER

Lord, ease my stress. Restore my life. Help me to enjoy life without being overburdened by turning to You. In choosing "less" burdens, I am really choosing "life" and my trust in You.

Amen.

17. THE BREAK

God was pouring a coffee for the young man.
It was time to have a break.
"How has it been so far?" asked God.
The young man looked at the Lord and shrugged his shoulders.
God merely waited…and listened.
We are all good at something…and this was God's Gift.

THOUGHTS

- God's silence does not mean God is not involved.
- God's silence is the wisdom of listening first.
- It is listening with the heart.
- The heart then responds as only the heart can…with compassion.
- God is a God of compassion.

PRAYER

God of Compassion and God of the Heart;
We know that You hear our every word, yet waiting for a response is sometimes frustrating.
We navigate our lives looking for signs that we are doing okay.
When we navigate our hearts, Lord, we are more aware of Your voice guiding us.
May we spend a portion of each day listening to the echoes of Your voice in our hearts. You give us hope that all will be well, even when our circumstances seem challenging or impossible.
Help us to hear Your voice in the silence of our heart.
For Your silence speaks volumes, Lord.

Amen.

18. STRENGTH

Strength is….

- Sometimes saying 'yes'.
- Sometimes saying 'no'.

Strength is…

- Staying confident.
- Looking at uncertainty in the face.
- Weeping with those who weep.

Strength is…

- Helping those who cannot help themselves.
- Sharing with those who have nothing.
- Trusting that all will be well.

Strength is…

- Remaining silent when tempted to speak.
- Speaking when tempted to remain silent.

…and being aware of God's Presence through it all is called… Wisdom.

PRAYER

Lord, it is sometimes difficult to know what to do in different situations.
Strength is valued but wisdom is valued even more.
Help us not to make rash decisions.
Help us to slow down our thoughts and situations we find ourselves in so that we can really think about decisions.
We ask that Your Spirit of Wisdom be with us every moment of our lives so that we can make good decisions.
For good decisions, Lord, is the true mark of strength.

Amen.

19. THE START OF COMPASSION - THROUGH A CHILD'S EYES

"Don't go outside," said the parent. "It is cold and wet."
With a pressed nose against the window pane, the child longingly peered out into the garden.
There were plenty of dark clouds and it was raining hard.
Leaves were blowing in the wind.
It was a stormy day.
Suddenly, the child saw a small, helpless baby bird on the ground.
Without a second thought, the child rushed to the door and opened it.
As the child struggled with the cold, wet weather, the baby bird was eventually scooped up and brought inside.
"Why risk your health for a tiny bird?" asked the parent. "You could get a cold and become sick!"
But God knew why the child did it.
Taking care of the defenceless creature was the real purpose.
God was in action through the compassion of the child!
And this is how God works…through our compassion and taking a risk ***with the heart.***

SCRIPTURE: **Matthew 20:29-34**

As Jesus and his disciples were leaving Jericho, a large crowd followed him.
Two blind men were sitting by the roadside, and when they heard that Jesus was going by, they shouted, "Lord, Son of David, have mercy on us!"
The crowd rebuked them and told them to be quiet, but they shouted all the louder, "Lord, Son of David, have mercy on us!"
Jesus stopped and called them. "What do you want me to do for you?" he asked.
"Lord," they answered, "we want our sight."
Jesus had compassion on them and touched their eyes. Immediately they received their sight and followed him.

Leader: The Gospel of the Lord.
All: **Praise to you, Lord Jesus Christ.**

20. IRREPLACEABLE CHILDREN'S MEMORIES

There are many memories that stay in the minds of children:

- the snuggling up to a loved pet
- the colour of beach sand
- the texture of Grandma's hair
- the smell of home-cooking
- a favourite book
- a favourite part of the playground
- a favourite outfit
- a favourite toy
- a special birthday (aren't they all special?)
- a special look
- a special word
- a special prayer.

God shares each moment with children.
God delights in these moments with children.
For God, these moments and moments with children are irreplaceable.

SCRIPTURE: Letter to the Colossians 3:12-15

Therefore, as God's chosen people, holy and dearly loved, clothe yourselves with compassion, kindness, humility, gentleness and patience.
Bear with each other and forgive one another if any of you has a grievance against someone. Forgive as the Lord forgave you. And over all these virtues put on love, which binds them all together in perfect unity.
Let the peace of Christ rule in your hearts, since as members of one body you were called to peace. And be thankful.

Leader: The Word of the Lord.
All: **Thanks be to God**.

PRAYER

Loving God, we thank you for our lives. We were made to grow in wisdom and to understand how much You love us. We pray that we will experience this understanding of Your love more and more each day. Help us to remember Your love in our lives each day.

Amen.

21. GREATNESS

The wise man looked at the crowd.
They had come to hear words of wisdom.
Someone from the crowd begged the question: "Wise one, what is ***greatness***?"
The wise sage thought about it in silence and eventually spoke:
"Greatness is not defined by victories or wealth. It is not determined by intelligence or status."
The crowd became curious.
Everything they knew about greatness pointed to power.
Yet this man defied what they all knew.
"Greatness is knowing the meaning of life for your soul…and then living it."
Jesus' wisdom was clear – he was truly wise.

THOUGHTS

- Life is not measured by 'things'.
- Life is measured by discovering what you are meant to do with life.
- Greatness is then having the courage to follow what you are meant to do.
- Holiness is having the courage to follow what God calls you to do.
- Greatness and holiness together is God's invitation to be fulfilled in life.
- The choice is ours.

SCRIPTURE: **John 8:31-32**

Jesus said,
"If you hold to my teaching, you are really my disciples. Then you will know the truth, and the truth will set you free."

Leader: The Gospel of the Lord.
All: **Praise to you, Lord Jesus Christ.**

22. HOW TO GROW A SOUL

Feed it wisdom.
Nurture the soul with affection.
Give it respect.
Demand integrity of it.
Move it with tears.
Tickle the soul with humour.
Embrace it with love.
Entrust the soul to God…and you will never doubt the worth of your soul.
For God **never** doubts the value of **your** soul.

PRAYER

Lord, the soul is precious.
Encourage us to keep our souls healthy.
Help us to expose our souls to the beauty of life.
For when our souls experience beauty, we experience You.

Amen.

SCRIPTURE: Psalm 121:2-3, 5-7

My help comes from the Lord, the Maker of Heaven and Earth.
He will not let your foot slip—He who watches over you will not sleep;
The Lord watches over you—the Lord is your shade at your right hand;
the sun will not harm you by day, nor the moon by night.
The Lord will keep you from all harm—He will watch over your life.

Leader: The Word of the Lord.
All: **Thanks be to God.**

23. A SIMPLE PRAYER

Lord,
May the day go gently.
May the speed of life not overwhelm life's travellers.
May anxiety not determine my spirit or my mood.
May tasks be done without stress or hurry.
May most expectations be fulfilled by this never-to-be-repeated day.
And may today be a simple, pleasant day;
Free from complexities or dramas and filled with peace and confidence.
For each day, Lord, brings with it the promise of Your support
in all that we do.

Amen.

SCRIPTURE: Psalm 131:1-2

My heart is not proud, Lord,
my eyes are not haughty.
I do not concern myself with great matters
or things too wonderful for me.
But I have calmed and quieted myself.
I am like a weaned child with its mother;
like a weaned child…I am content.

Leader: The Word of the Lord.
All: **Thanks be to God.**

24. GOD NEVER FORGETS

God never forgets:
- our acts of kindness
- our treasured moments
- our wins
- our defeats.

God always wants to know:
- what matters to us
- what consoles us
- what inspires us
- what annoys us.

God never mentions:
- weaknesses
- temptations
- negative feelings

God never puts down…but God always raises up…
Our positive words and encouragement towards others makes God proud of us.
For *then* we become the face of God…the face of kindness, of inspiration and of consolation.
We *then* become the face of God.

SCRIPTURE: Hebrews 6:10-11

God is not unjust;
God will not forget your work and the love you have shown Him,
as you have helped His people.

Leader: The Word of the Lord.
All: **Thanks be to God.**

25. FUNCTIONING WELL

Her child was functioning well.
Her child was settled and calm.
Her child was easy to handle.
This meant that the parent was functioning well.
His child was not functioning well.
His child was unsettled and angry.
His child was hard to handle.
This meant that the parent was not functioning well.
Whatever happens in the lives of the people we love, affects us.
God loves us.
God is affected by what happens in our lives.
God wants us to function well.
It is a function that God treasures…our wellbeing…and God promises to help us always with it.

SCRIPTURE: Psalm 119:10, 18, 30, 34, 37, 41, 49

Response: I seek You with all my heart; Lord.

I seek You with all my heart; Lord.
Open my eyes that I may see wonderful things in Your law.
Response: I seek You with all my heart; Lord.

I have chosen the way of faithfulness; I have set my heart on Your laws.
Give me understanding, so that I may keep Your law
and obey it with all my heart.
Response: I seek You with all my heart; Lord.

Turn my eyes away from worthless things;
May Your unfailing love come to me, Lord,
…for You have given me hope.
Response: I seek You with all my heart; Lord.

26. SOMETHING GOOD

The wise man approached the parent of a young family.
"Tell me something good that's happening in your life," asked the wise man.
And so he heard about the birth of children and the hopes and dreams of a bright future.
The wise man continued his journey. He came across a young person walking along the road.
"Tell me something good that's happening in your life," asked the wise man.
And so he heard about moving to a new country and the hopes and dreams of a better future.
The wise man continued his journey. He came across a young man.
"Tell me something good that's happening in your life," asked the wise man.
And the young man told him enthusiastically what changes the future would bring because of the power of love and forgiveness.
Then the wise man shook his head and asked
"How do you know this? What is your name?"
And the young man told him his name. They continued to travel together for a while.
The young man was going towards a town called Cana where there was a wedding feast. His name?
It was Jesus.

THOUGHTS

- Love changes everything.
- Love sharpens the focus.
- Love deepens the understanding.
- Love changes everything.
- God is love.

PRAYER

Loving God, Your nature is pure love.
Help us to remember this
when other understandings get in the way.

Amen.

27. LISTENING TO GOD

The young woman prayed:
"Lord, how do I learn to hear Your voice? How do I listen?"
And God replied. In the deep silence, she heard no human words but...
Her heart began to stir.
Her heart began to soften.
She was listening to God...and hearing God's voice through the movements in her heart.

THOUGHTS

- Words can communicate.
- But so does music.
- And art.
- And joy.
- And tears.
- God uses all of these to communicate... by moving the heart.

SCRIPTURE

You are my portion, Lord;
I have promised to obey Your words.
I have sought Your face with all my heart. (Psalm 119:57-58)

Your hands made me and formed me;
give me understanding to learn Your commands. (Psalm 119:73)

May Your unfailing love be my comfort. (Psalm 76)
Let Your compassion come to me that I may live. (Psalm 119:77)

28. GOD KNOWS

God knows what make us tick.
God knows what makes us come alive.
God knows why we are here on earth.
When we understand all of this, we understand ourselves better… and we understand God ***much*** better.

SCRIPTURE

Your word is a lamp for my feet,
a light on my path. (Psalm 119:105)

You are my refuge and my shield;
I have put my hope in Your word (Psalm 119; 114)

Sustain me, my God, according to Your promise, and I will live;
do not let my hopes be dashed (Psalm 119:116)

The unfolding of Your words gives light;
it gives understanding to the simple. (Psalm 119:130)

Turn to me and have mercy on me,
as You always do to those who love Your name. (Psalm 119:132)

PRAYER

Lord of All Life, You understand our thoughts and our hopes
even before we utter them.
Continue to be our strength in times of struggle.
Guide us in the right way.
Protect us from all harm.
And show us how to truly live.

Amen.

29. THE SECRET TO A COMPLICATED LIFE

Lord, life can be complicated.

- When I say 'yes' but I mean 'no'.
- When I promise to deliver but know I really can't.
- When my time is little but the demands are great.
- When I say it wrong instead of saying it right.
- When I react rather than act.
- When I rush rather than relax.
- When I forget rather than remember.
- When I give my attention to other matters rather than to You.

Lord, each day has its own potential to become complicated.
It doesn't take much.
Circumstances change.
People change.
But You, Lord, are a steady rock.
Be the foundation of all that I say and do today.

Amen.

SCRIPTURE: Mark 12:13-17

Later they sent some of the Pharisees and Herodians to Jesus to catch him in his words. They came to him and said, "Teacher, we know that you are a man of integrity. You aren't swayed by others, because you pay no attention to who they are; but you teach the way of God in accordance with the truth. Is it right to pay the imperial tax to Caesar or not? Should we pay or shouldn't we?"
But Jesus knew their hypocrisy. "Why are you trying to trap me?" he asked. "Bring me a denarius and let me look at it." They brought the coin, and he asked them, "Whose image is this? And whose inscription?"
"Caesar's," they replied.
Then Jesus said to them, "Give back to Caesar what is Caesar's and to God what is God's."
And they were amazed at him.

Leader: The Gospel of the Lord.
All: **Praise to you, Lord Jesus Christ.**

30. THE PERFECT CHILD

God was about to create the perfect child.
"What will be the most important feature of the perfect child?" asked one of the angels.
God paused and thought about it deeply.
God finally answered.
"To create the perfect child," said God, "I will first create a heart that loves another person deeply, other than My own."
And with that, God created parents first.
For God knew that every parent had the 'perfect child' – their child.

SCRIPTURE: Mark 12:28-31

One of the teachers of the law came and heard them debating. Noticing that Jesus had given them a good answer, he asked him, "Of all the commandments, which is the most important?"
"The most important one" answered Jesus, "is this:
'Hear, O Israel: The Lord our God, the Lord is one. Love the Lord your God with all your heart and with all your soul and with all your mind and with all your strength.'
The second is this: 'Love your neighbour as yourself.'
There is no commandment greater than these."

Leader: The Gospel of the Lord.
All: **Praise to you, Lord Jesus Christ.**

PRAYER

Lord, we thank you for the gift of children.
May we always teach them that in Your eyes, they are perfect
and treasured forever.
May all children come to know You and always love You in return
with all their soul and mind and strength. For in doing this, they will be encouraged to love all people
You created too, with the same love.

Amen.

31. TRUTH

The woman went shopping.
She wanted to buy something called 'truth'.
"We don't have any in stock at the moment," said a sales assistant. "I can order it in for you, but it may take a few weeks. If you need it urgently, I suggest you go online."
And so she did.
She typed in the word 'truth'.
The search engine went nuts.
There were millions of websites dedicated to 'truth'.
It was confusing!
Each website had its own version of 'truth'.
But the important question for her was: 'what is ***God's*** Truth?'

THOUGHTS

- God treasures Truth.
- Nothing else matters to God.
- Sometimes the truth is challenging.
- But the truth that really matters is the kind that sets you *free.*

PRAYER

God of Truth,
God of Sincerity,
God of Life,
God of Compassion.
Help us to understand the kind of truth that will help us to become whole.
Amen.

32. THE GOOD TEACHER DAY

Lord, today was a good day.
But it wasn't the kind of 'good' day by everyone's standards.
It was a good day because:

- A child in my class finally learnt how to do shoelaces.
- All of my students were nice to each other for most of the day.
- Parents offered to go with me and the children on that difficult school excursion.
- I managed to have a great yard duty.
- A parent thanked me at the end of the day.
- A colleague paid me an unexpected compliment.
- Every bit of technology in the classroom worked a treat!
- My students went home happy.
- The staff meeting finished a little earlier than anticipated.

Lord, I thank you for a smooth and uneventful day.
I thank you for the peace that surrounds me when the day is positive.
And we both know, Lord, that people in my life notice my 'good days'.
For the Grace that I experience on a 'good' day, glows inside of me for others to see.
Thank you, Lord, for a good day and for the peace in my heart that it brings.
This kind of joy is worthwhile.
It is Your gift to me; an assurance that tells me this is how school life is meant to be.
Thank you, Lord.

Amen.

SCRIPTURE: Psalm 146:2

I will praise the Lord all my life;
I will sing praise to my God as long as I live.

Leader: The Word of the Lord.
All: **Thanks be to God.**

33. THE STUDENT WIN

He had been pretty good kid. Everyone knew it.
Then he "went off the rails" a bit because of something someone had said to him.
He cried on the inside…and no-one suspected it.
He couldn't concentrate…and others could tell the change in him.
Then he got mad…but made a positive choice about it.
Instead of reacting badly and taking it out on others, he worked through how he felt.
He realised he could choose to win or lose, depending on how he reacted.
In the end, he won. He knew it. Others knew it.
How?
He didn't react.
He only responded.
There is a difference.

THOUGHTS

- God does not react.
- No matter how bad the situation gets.
- God responds.
- There is a difference.

PRAYER

God of the persecuted, of the disempowered and of the misunderstood:
Through the humanity of Jesus, You understood those who were frustrated by injustice. You have a special place for those who respond to frustration with dignity and peace.
May Your Holy Spirit continue to inspire all who are committed to Your ways of responding in peaceful ways.

Amen..

34. THE FIRST DAY BACK AT SCHOOL

Dear Staff Member, (anyone who works in a school)
I am your student.
You may not know me yet, but I have already heard a few things about you.
We are going to be together in a new learning environment and I have mixed emotions about it.
Some days I worry about how we are going to get along; but I come to you full of hopes and dreams.
I hope you will learn as much about me as I intend to learn about you.
But I need to share some things with you about me.

- My nervousness will sometimes get the better of me.
- When I am put on the spot, I can't find or say the right words to express myself.
- Then I may smirk nervously or even come across as not-caring. I understand this response may irritate you.
- And when I open my mouth to explain what happened to attract your attention, I may miss some of the information I need to give you.

Believe me! I know I can disappoint you and myself should this happen.
Please don't think I want to upset you on purpose.
Yes, there will be days when I don't feel like learning or listening. But we both hope those days will be few.
What I really hope is that you will like me.
When I sense this, I will surprise you and myself at how ambitious I become to learn or be more open to what you have to say to me.
And thank you for turning up day after day to spend your valuable time with me.
I look forward to the journey ahead and trust that your skills will help me see the journey through *your* eyes.
Thank you for having understood a bit about me through *my* eyes.
Now... let's get on with the job of understanding each other and continuing the journey through ***God's eyes.***

PRAYER

Lord, we pray for a good start to the year. Help us help our students to become the best they can be, by our own best efforts to help them. Guide us in all of our dealings with young people.

Amen.

35. THE GREAT SCHOOL DAY

It was the end of a school day.
It had been a great day!
Everything had gone well: lessons, assemblies and student meetings.
The teachers knew it.
The kids knew it.
The principal knew it.
And it had little to do with learning great amounts of content in the classroom.
...it had everything to do with how people had treated each other.
How have people been treated today?
Our way?
Or God's way?

THOUGHTS

- God knows what will bring us happiness.
- God knows what will bring us peace.
- Knowledge about happiness is important.
- Knowledge about peace is important.
- But it is in the "doing" that makes it real to God and to others.

PRAYER

Lord,
Thank you for those seamless, beautiful days when all goes well.
Thank you for the joy we experience when people cooperate respectfully.
Thank you for the surreal feeling we get of "everything's going to be okay" days that flow peacefully and serenely.
You give us hope. You give us peace. You, Lord, make our day.
Thank you for caring about us.

Amen.

36. HAPPY-HAPPY GOD

God was laughing.
God was tickled pink.
God was trying hard to suppress a giggle.
But then God burst out loud into gales of laughter.
And God continued to smile.
God was happy.
'Why are you so happy?" asked a curious young child. This was not the God people had imagined.
God smiled....and smiled...and then laughed...and laughed
The laughter was infectious!
The child couldn't help but join in.
Together they laughed until there were tears streaming down their faces!
Why?
...Because God was happy.

THOUGHTS

- God is found in the ordinary experience; a warm smile, a good laugh, a humorous moment.
- This is what makes God so extraordinary.
- God is closer to us than we realise.
- Look for the ordinary moments of joy and experience God.

PRAYER

Lord, we discover more about ourselves through our laughter than through our tears.
May we always remember to seek happiness. Surround us with people who will make us laugh and enjoy life.
Help us to be positive in our outlook, for in doing so, we become Your people of hope.

Amen.

37. THE POWERFUL WORDS

The wise old man sat and just listened.
A crowd had come to see him and hear the wisdom of his words.
"Wise one," they asked him, "tell us what are the most powerful words in the world are?"
The wise man pondered on the question.
Eventually he answered, "The most powerful words are 'I forgive you'".
People nodded in agreement.
"Now tell us," they quizzed him, "what are most destructive words in the world?"
Without hesitation the wise man answered,
"The most destructive words are 'I will ***never*** forgive you.'"

THOUGHTS

- God does not understand the words "I will never forgive you."
- God's nature forgives each time we ask.
- Another word for forgiveness is 'love'.
- For whoever forgives, loves.
- And whoever loves, forgives.
- It's that simple.

SCRIPTURE: Psalm 130:1-5

Out of the depths I cry to you, Lord;
Lord, hear my voice.
Let your ears be attentive
to my cry for mercy.
If you, Lord, kept a record of sins,
Lord, who could stand?
But with you there is forgiveness,
so that we can, with reverence, serve you.
I wait for the Lord; my whole being waits,
and in the Lord's word I put my hope.

38. WHAT REALLY MAKES MY DAY AT SCHOOL

Lord, today has been a good day.
- My marking is up to date.
- The principal remembered my name.
- I kept up with my emails.
- I remembered to do my yard duty *all week*.

But, Lord, we know that a good day is not always about ***me.***
It is a good day when:
- The kids get along.
- The lessons run smoothly.
- My students get top marks for my test.
- I don't argue with them (and if I do, we agree to disagree: win-win!)

Lord, we both know that it is a good day when the results are not about me…but the outcomes are focused on others.
For when we care about having a good day, it is usually about how all the other people in our lives affect us and our world.
Help us to have a good day over and over again.

Amen.

SCRIPTURE: 3 John 1:2, 5, 6, 11.

Dear friend, I pray that you may enjoy good health and that all may go well with you.
You are faithful in what you are doing for the brothers and sisters, even though they are strangers to you.
We ought therefore to show hospitality to such people so that we may work together for the truth.
Dear friend, do not imitate what is evil but what is good. Anyone who does what is good is from God.

Leader: The Word of the Lord.
All: **Thanks be to God.**

39. SEVEN SIGNS OF HAPPINESS FOR CHILDREN

1. Watching a very young child hold a pencil and trying to write their name without help.
2. Hearing a five-year old say 'Bless you!" after you sneeze and then brings you a crumpled tissue.
3. Observing a young child patiently wait their turn to play in the sand pit.
4. Listening to a wide-eyed youngster tell you about how worried they are about their sick pet.
5. Being amazed when two young children apologise to each other.
6. Cherishing that first card you receive from a parent to say 'thank you'.
7. Attaching importance to the first time a young child works out how to tie shoe laces.

Then you know you have the privilege of being…a teacher!

THOUGHTS

- Happiness is possible for everyone.
- God wants us to experience happiness in the ordinary achievements of life.
- If we can do this, then God's joy is complete.
- Choose happiness.

SCRIPTURE: 1 John 5:2-3, 14-15

This is how we know that we love the children of God: by loving God and carrying out his commands. In fact, this is love for God: to keep his commands.
This is the confidence we have in approaching God: that if we ask anything according to his will, he hears us. And if we know that he hears us—whatever we ask—we know that we have what we asked of him.

Leader: The Word of the Lord.
All: **Thanks be to God.**

PRAYER

Lord, as people working in schools, we are lucky to watch our students conquer important milestones in their development. May they carry into the future a spirit of determination to follow their dreams and goals.

Amen.

40. THANK YOU, LORD, FOR LAUGHTER

Lord, thank you for the gift of laughter:
For all the interesting cackles that delight (or mildly irritate)

- For the giggles that are infectious and put us in a good mood
- For the unique, explosive laughter that you cannot ignore
- For the quiet, muffled, low kind of laughter that captures your attention
- For the belly-jiggling laughter that causes tears to run down your face
- For the hearty 'ho ho haa haa ho haa haa' laughter that you cannot ignore
- For the spontaneous laughter that exposes a beautiful smile
- For the joker's laughter that announces innocent mischief
- For the laughter that can only be expressed by a happy face
- For the laughter that says 'I like you'
- And the laughter that invites the unspoken request: 'can we be friends?'

Lord, thank you for all the different kinds of laughter that link us to each other.
You created laughter the same time that You created love.
May we experience moments of humour today. Those moments have the capacity to re-ignite our spirit and passion for life…Your gifts to us.

Amen.

THOUGHTS

Laughter is universal

- …irrespective of time, age, status or place.
- God can be found in laughter
- …for God is found everywhere
- …irrespective of time, age, status or place.
- Laugh.
- Let laughter touch your spirit.
- And your spirit will be restored.

SCRIPTURE: Psalm 16:9, 11

…my heart is glad and my tongue rejoices;
You make known to me the path of life;
you will fill me with joy in your presence…

Leader: The Word of the Lord.
All: **Thanks be to God.**

41. COMMUNICATION AND STRENGTH

They were laughing together: the mobile went off.
They were arguing: the mobile went off.
They were talking pleasantly: the mobile went off.
They were in a meeting: the mobile went off.
They were resting: the mobile went off.
Each time, the mobile sat firmly at its place at the table – like an old friend.
It travels intimately with us, wherever we go.
We regularly steal glances at the screen…in case we miss something.
Sometimes, it has no manners when it goes off.
It is desired.
It is depended upon.
It speaks.
It commands.
It rules.
They were praying: the mobile went off and then it was…turned off.
What strength!

SCRIPTURE: 1 Corinthians 7:21-23

Were you a slave when you were called (by God)? Don't let it trouble you—although if you can gain your freedom, do so.
For the one who was a slave when called to faith in the Lord is the Lord's freed person; similarly, the one who was free when called is Christ's slave.
You were bought at a price; do not become slaves of human beings.

Leader: The Word of the Lord.
All: **Thanks be to God.**

42. THE TEXT

The text read:
"I'm sorry."
A text response came back.
It read:
"I forgive you."
Which response was more effective?

THOUGHTS

- To forgive is to begin a relationship again.
- When one person forgives, the other person is given more than just forgiveness.
- The other person is given hope.
- For that is the gift of forgiveness: hope.
- And hope is a precious, precious gift.
- God always forgives: God is hope.

PRAYER

Lord, in Your eyes, to hope has only one option: to forgive.
We sometimes doubt that forgiving others is possible.
But for You, Lord, forgiveness is never a doubt....
...it is ***the*** solution.
Help us to have the courage to seek reconciliation.
Help us to see hopeful situations with fresh eyes.
Help us to not ignore the yearning to seek peace.
For in seeking peace, we are seeking a tranquil heart and a mind that is at ease.
This is the gift You give us...hope.

Amen.

43. AN AMUSING KIND OF DAY

Lord, some days are kind of amusing.
- I receive interesting emails that provoke me into laughter or irritation.
- I get the wrong message or the wrong interpretation of what is going on around me.
- I get confused about who wants what, when and how.
(Then I get told that it was supposed to have happened yesterday!)
- The end-of-year Staff Christmas Lunch Planning Party can never satisfy everyone.
- The Sports Day Committee is hampered with Occupational Health and Safety issues.
- The staffroom clean-up roster becomes a political hot-potato.
- **Who** sits **where** in the staff room can compromise one's career aspirations.
- A new idea put forward becomes too hard, too soft, too easy or too creative.
- You, Lord, sometimes don't get a mention during staff prayer.
- What was a 'sure thing' yesterday becomes 'unsure everything' today.
Lord, I ask You to help me be patient when my days are 'amusing'.
Give me a positive perspective on it all.
Guide my spirit to understand what is really going on and to end each day with the hope that it will all get sorted by the morning.

Amen.

SCRIPTURE: **Proverbs 27:1-2**

Do not boast about tomorrow,
for you do not know what a day may bring.
Let someone else praise you, and not your own mouth;
an outsider, and not your own lips.

Leader: The Gospel of the Lord.
All: **Praise to you, Lord Jesus Christ**.

44. HOW TO DE-CLUTTER

Her space was full of clutter.
The clutter covered every bit of wall and floor space.
Everywhere she looked, she saw the chaos.
What a burden!
Eventually, she couldn't stand it any longer and decided to call a removalist.
There was a knock on the door.
As she opened the door to let the removalist in, she recognised the person: it was Jesus.
"Why don't you let me organise all of this? It won't take me long," he suggested to her.
It was all she needed to hear.
She was looking forward to simplifying it all with Jesus.

THOUGHTS

- Life tends to attract clutter.
- Our minds.
- Our hearts.
- Our souls.
- Sometimes we need to 'de-clutter' to feel in control again.
- Jesus can 'de-clutter' our hearts and souls: but we must invite him in.
- Then all we need to do is **trust.**

PRAYER

Lord, it is easy to overload ourselves with too many thoughts, too many ideas and too many decisions.
When we do this, we feel pressed for time and we are under pressure.
Our humanity and our sense of joy change and we become 'short' or upset with ourselves and with others.
Help us to stay balanced and not cram in too much activity into our lives.
Help us to say 'no' with wisdom.
And when it gets too much, Lord, remind us to keep still and wait for Your Presence.

Amen.

45. THE PROBLEM OF UNDERSTANDING

The angels and the saints were gathered together for a conference.
God was the key-note speaker.
All were inspired by God's Words!
During question time, one little angel brought before God a concern about how humanity was conducting itself on Earth.
"Lord," asked the curious angel "why do You keep giving humans so many chances and keep wanting them back?"
The Lord merely gazed at them all with enormous love and replied,
"It's because **I understand**."

THOUGHTS

- To love is to understand.
- To have compassion is to understand.
- God knows only this: to have compassion for us
- For it is the greatest kind of love.

SCRIPTURE: 2 Timothy 1:9

He has saved us and called us to a holy life—not because of anything we have done but because of his own purpose and grace.
This grace was given us in Christ Jesus before the beginning of time.

Leader: The Word of the Lord.
All: **Thanks be to God.**

46. WHAT IS MEANT TO BE

Sometimes…
Sometimes…just sometimes…the traffic jam happens for a purpose.
Sometimes the phone rings and you can't answer it.
Sometimes the flight is delayed.
Sometimes the story is not fully told.
Sometimes the words are not spoken.
The mysteries of life run deep.
Sometimes, it is better that there is a delay of some sort because it may be God's attempt to keep you safe.
And the mystery deepens when…

- people come into your life.
- people move out of your life.

A task has been finished.
A hope has been accomplished.
A Plan has been fulfilled.
You never know for sure why things happen. But they do.
The idea is to rely on God for an outcome that will bring hope and peace.

THOUGHTS

- Life is a mystery.
- God does not allow us to know the future.
- God just encourages us to trust that all will be well.
- Trust.

PRAYER

Lord, often we have plans. Sometimes our plans don't go according to plan. Only You, Lord, know the reasons for this. May we always trust in You. Keep us safe from harm…always.

Amen.

47. IF...

If the world's problems were solved there would be:

- no wars
- no hunger
- no injustice

If wars and hunger and injustice were eliminated from the world there would only be one quality left: love.
If love is not enough to save the world, then ***nothing*** is enough.
...because love is another word for 'hope'.
And another word for 'hope' is God.

SCRIPTURE: Proverbs 25:21-22

If your enemy is hungry, give him food to eat;
if he is thirsty, give him water to drink.
In doing this...the Lord will reward you.

Leader: The Word of the Lord.
All: **Thanks be to God.**

PRAYER

Jesus, during your earthly ministry, You repeated Your message about having hope over and over again.
Our world is suffering from the effects of climate change and global warming. It suffers from disempowerment to protect the vulnerable. It crumbles under the impact of exploitation. We ask that our efforts to protect creation, begin with a love for all creation, including our vulnerable brothers and sisters in the world. May we always remember to give generously to the efforts of reconciliation and protection, especially those who are threatened with destruction of any kind.

Amen.

48. IF ONLY I...

Lord,
I think about today and I come to a number of conclusions.
If only:

- I had woken up and been a bit more positive.
- I had said 'yes' instead of 'no'.
- I had listened more instead of talking too much.
- I had not put forward my opinion so strongly about a delicate matter.
- I had planned a bit of 'me' time during the course of the day.
- I hadn't been so bossy with my friends.
- I taken the day off as mum had suggested.

But, Lord, I am *only five years old* and have just had my first full week at school.
Help me to cope with life at school (they tell me it will be with me a long, long time!)
You know I get tired a lot and then become easily distracted.
I hope next week will be a better week for all of us, Lord. I know you understand.

Amen.

THOUGHTS

- Our days can get busier and not slower.
- Young children don't always cope with the fast pace of life.
- They say or do unreasonable things when this happens.
- God offers them a balance in their busy young lives.
- This balance is called: **prayer.**

SCRIPTURE: Mark 1:35-37

Very early in the morning, while it was still dark, Jesus got up, left the house and went off to a solitary place, where he prayed.
Simon and his companions went to look for him, and when they found him, they exclaimed: "Everyone is looking for you!"

Leader: The Gospel of the Lord.
All: **Praise to you, Lord Jesus Christ**.

49. THE YEAR-LEVEL MEETING AND GIFTS

Lord, before we begin this meeting, we remember all the students we came into contact with today. In their own way they are gifts. We remember:

- The ones who were late to school.
- The ones who were in a bad mood.
- The ones who played fairly on the oval or on the playground equipment.
- The ones who tackled others during a game when they were reminded for the hundredth time that tackling was not acceptable.
- We remember the ones who muttered under their breath.
- The ones who cried and wouldn't say why.
- We remember the ones who cried and over-exaggerated what *really* happened.
- We remember the beautiful, thoughtful projects done by committed and talented students.
- We also remember the lame excuses from those who didn't get the project done on time.
- We remember the children who wore their uniform with pride.
- We also remember the children who struggled to know what the word 'pride' means.
- We remember the distress of those younger children who missed out on classroom birthday invitations.
- We remember the funny moments, the sacred moments and the prayerful moments.

Lord, thank you for all these experiences.
However, Lord, we ask that You spread these experiences out evenly over the course of the week. It is tough to have them all happen all at once before midday!
But we know, Lord, that if it happens again, we can always turn to You for guidance and strength. Lord, give us strength…for tomorrow.
Amen.

SCRIPTURE: 1 Corinthians 12:4-11

There are different kinds of gifts, but the same Spirit distributes them. There are different kinds of service, but the same Lord. There are different kinds of working, but in all of them and in everyone it is the same God at work.

Now to each one the manifestation of the Spirit is given for the common good.

To one there is given through the Spirit a message of wisdom, to another a message of knowledge by means of the same Spirit, to another faith by the same Spirit, to another gifts of healing by that one Spirit, to another miraculous powers, to another prophecy, to another distinguishing between spirits, to another speaking in different kinds of tongues, and to still another the interpretation of tongues.

All these are the work of one and the same Spirit, and he distributes them to each one, just as he determines.

Leader: The Word of the Lord.
All: **Thanks be to God.**

50. WOMAN

Lord, I am a woman.
I am a question and an answer.
I can be a comedian or very serious.
I can be a problem-solver and a problem-creator all at once.
I give life to others, even if this does not include birth.
I am a story teller and a story-seeker.
My mind is sometimes obsessed with staying busy.
Occasionally I am brilliant!
I can nurture. I can listen.
I enjoy hearing my words.
I am a thought-thinker. I support.
I know how to grieve: that lost opportunity or that lost person.
I synergise, I regenerate and I renew.
And when I don't, others can tell.
I can connect with the disconnected.
I also know how to disconnect with the connected.
I am an argument-settler or an argument-starter.
I am enough…and more.
I am…complicated sometimes.
Yet God created me to be ***me***…and not anyone else.
I thank God for me and for all of the gifts I have.
Blessed be the Lord of all creation!

SCRIPTURE: Genesis 1:31

God saw all that God had made, and it was very good.